Howard
DEAN

In His Own Words

Howard
DEAN

In His Own Words

EDITED BY LISA ROGAK

Thomas Dunne Books/St. Martin's Griffin ⚇ New York

THOMAS DUNNE BOOKS.
An imprint of St. Martin's Press.

www.stmartins.com

ISBN 0-312-33073-1

10 9 8 7 6 5 4 3 2

CONTENTS

INTRODUCTION

The first thing you should know about Howard Dean is that he has never lost an election since he first ran for office in 1982. An impressive accomplishment, considering that the only elected positions he has held were in Vermont, a notoriously liberal state where those on the left frequently accused Dean of being a conservative, while those on the right got along with him just fine, as long as he stuck to business issues.

Since Dr. Dean first appeared on the national political radar in the spring of 2002, he has been frequently misinterpreted. This is understandably easy to do, since Dean has never adhered to set party platforms or straight-ticket politics.

Although the media, his fellow Democratic candidates, and Republicans alike are painting Dean as a card-carrying liberal, those who knew him as governor say he's being mislabeled. As Tom Salmon, a former Democratic two-term governor of Vermont, put it, "His being called a liberal is one of the great white lies of the campaign. He's a rock-solid fiscal conservative and a liberal on key social issues."

It's hard to deny the buzz growing around the former governor. Howard Dean's campaign raised $7.6 million in the second quarter of 2003, far surpassing his fellow Democratic candidates, and he did it primarily through his Web site. As of September 2003, almost a quarter-million people from all fifty states have signed up to volunteer for the campaign. In late August, when the governor made a campaign swing through the Pacific Northwest, fifteen thousand people showed up to hear him speak in Seattle; only four thousand were expected. The frenzy among the audience at his campaign appearances feels like a rock concert, and has even led one reporter to compare Dean to a rock star.

These accomplishments have created plenty of hype around the candidate, but most people still don't know where Dean stands on the issues, sound bites aside.

Like many Americans, I'm disillusioned with the state

of American politics today. Especially since I live in New Hampshire, where we're been listening to almost-daily reports for two years now on which potential primary candidates have been tramping across the state. It takes a lot for these cookie-cutter candidates to stand out. Of course, they usually don't, so most people in the state have learned to tune them out.

From all indications, Dean is different. He speaks his mind, answers questions directly, and admits he doesn't know something when he—surprise!—doesn't know. In state and national politics, this is a novelty.

You can use *Howard Dean: In His Own Words* to learn where the former governor stands on the issues that matter most to Americans today and to help decide if Howard Dean is the right candidate for you.

HOWARD DEAN IN BRIEF

Howard Dean was born in New York City in 1954 and grew up on Park Avenue. His father was a stockbroker. His mother is an art appraiser who still lives in Manhattan.

He graduated with a BA from Yale University in 1971. After college, he spent a year as a ski bum in Aspen, before moving back East to work on Wall Street as a stockbroker for about a year. Dean decided his heart wasn't in finance, and so he attended the Albert Einstein College of Medicine in New York City. He earned his medical degree in 1978, the same year he moved to Vermont. Judith Steinberg, whom he met in medical school, followed him north shortly after. They were married in 1981 and established a joint medical practice in Shelburne, just south of Burlington, the state's largest city.

Dean ran for representative to the Vermont House in 1982, a position he held until 1986, when he was elected lieutenant governor. During that time, he continued to practice medicine, since the only elected office in state government requiring a full-time commitment is the governor.

One day in the summer of 1991, Dr. Dean was in the middle of examining a patient when he received word that then-Governor Richard Snelling had suddenly died of a heart attack. He finished the exam and headed for Montpelier to take the oath of office to finish out Snelling's term. He served the next five two-year terms as governor until 2002, when he decided not to run in order to pursue his bid for the Democratic nomination for the 2004 presidential election.

Howard
DEAN

In His Own Words

On Affirmative Action

Human beings tend to be most comfortable with people like ourselves. And there's nothing wrong with that, but when it comes to jobs and education, if there isn't affirmative action, people will keep on choosing people just like themselves, and that cuts off a lot of opportunity— for society and for the people who don't get picked.

LA Weekly, August 29, 2003

———

This country is more diverse than any on earth; soon there will not be a majority. That is not going to cut it for this country. We need to make sure we all work together regardless of your background.

Iowa City Press-Citizen, January 20, 2003

———

On Agriculture

Ultimately, I think that we need to change how we subsidize and help agriculture. I don't think we should put limits on production, but we can put limits on how much is helped by the farm bill.

Meet the Press, July 21, 2002

————

On Americans

There's no such thing as a boring American.

LA Weekly, August 29, 2003

————

Average Americans, who are concerned with working and feeding their families and are not that interested in politics, think [his fellow Democratic candidates] are a bunch of politicians who don't have much to say. Average Americans vote for the person they like, and they vote for the person they trust.

U.S. News & World Report, August 11, 2003

———

Americans want to hear from someone who's not timid about the direction the country should take, and is not about nuances and shades of difference.

The Guardian, August 27, 2002

———

The Americans I have met love their country. They believe deeply in its promise, our values and our principles. But they know something is wrong and they want to take action. They want to do something to right our path. But they feel Washington isn't listening. And as individuals, they lack the power to change the course those in Washington have put us on.

"Great American Restoration" speech, June 23, 2003

———

On Balancing the Budget

I'm one of the more progressive people in the race while still being a moderate at home, because if you believe in a balanced budget, that automatically disqualifies you from being a Progressive [in Vermont]. And I think at the national level, that's not true.

The Nation, March 31, 2003

———

The fact is no Republican has balanced the budget for thirty-four years. If you want fiscal responsibility and you want somebody who is going to balance the budget, you're going to have to elect a Democrat, because Republicans don't do that—they can't manage money.

Concord Monitor, January 24, 2003

———

If you want social justice in this country, you have to be able to handle the books, you must be able to balance the budget.

Iowa City Press-Citizen, January 20, 2003

———

On Being a Physician

I'm not running for president in spite of the fact that I'm a doctor. In a very real sense, I'm running because of it.

Speech, Columbia University, May 13, 2003

———

The good thing about being a doctor is that you are results-oriented. Facts are very important. I used to be against needle-exchange programs, because I thought they might spread addiction. Then the Yale studies came out around 1993 and 1994, and I changed my position almost overnight. Sometimes I get impatient with emotional arguments that are not based on anything. I like to cut to the chase.

The Nation, March 31, 2003

———

Sympathy and support is what patients need. You have to tell them the truth. If they have cancer, you can't say "This is not a big deal." You say "You have the possibility for a reasonable length of life, and here's what we're going to do"—bang, bang, bang. Most people don't appreciate uncertainty. And that is my job as a presidential candidate, to inspire confidence and empower people to believe in themselves.

The Washington Post, August 4, 2003

————

The three things I liked best [in medical school] were psychiatry, surgery, and medicine. I decided against surgery, which I love, because I didn't want to be married to the hospital. And I decided against psychiatry, because I didn't think I could listen to everybody's problems eight hours a day. Which, of course, is what I do now. Except it's thirteen hours a day.

U.S. News & World Report, August 11, 2003

———

That's what the job is. That's what physicians are inherently required to do in the course of their work . . . to accurately assess and analyze data, in order to reach a diagnosis and a plan of treatment.

Dean on applying doctor skills to political office
LA Weekly, August 29, 2003

———

On Being Called a Liberal

I think it's pathetic that I'm considered the left-wing liberal. It shows just how far to the right this country has lurched.

The Washington Post, July 6, 2003

———

I don't believe in giving away the store. I'm not an old-fashioned 1960s liberal.

Vermont Public Radio news report, March 20, 2003

———

If being a liberal means a balanced budget, I'm a liberal. If being a liberal means adding jobs instead of subtracting them, then please, call me a liberal.

The New York Times, July 30, 2003

———

When I ran for reelection in Vermont, I won with 40 percent of the Republican vote and 60 percent of the independent vote.

PoliticsNJ.com, June 6, 2002

———

The Progressives hate me because they're all big liberals and I'm not. I've stopped them [from raising taxes] on many occasions.

The Nation, March 31, 2003

———

I don't really consider myself a Progressive, though by national standards maybe I am.

The Nation, March 31, 2003

———

I have trouble with the liberal wing of my own party.

The State, March 5, 2002

———

Anybody who labels me as an ultraliberal is probably right-wing. Those are the people we need to get out of office. I'm only too happy to take them on. If balancing the budget for twelve years in a row—and the Republicans are incapable of doing that—is being liberal, then I think it's time for a liberal comeback.

The Stranger, May 15, 2003

———

These guys think they're getting a raving liberal. And then they find out I'm not a raving liberal. I'm kind of in the middle and, for example, I'm in favor of workfare. Then they don't know what to say. All the questions they've carefully written down to fry me go out the window.

The Washington Post, July 31, 2003

———

On the Bush Tax Cuts

These tax cuts are incredibly bad for the economy. I believe their purpose is essentially to defund the federal government so that Medicare and Social Security, the icons of the New Deal, will be undone.

Meet the Press, June 22, 2003

———

The good thing about the president's tax cut is that $1.6 billion will fund an awful lot [if it's eliminated].

The New Republic, July 1, 2002

———

I don't have anything against giving people tax cuts, but we can't afford tax cuts right now and our party ought to stand up and say so.

Barre–Montpelier Vermont "The Times Argus," April 2, 2003

———

I saw the president complain that the Democrats were talking about class warfare. But I really think it's the president that's practicing class warfare, because all of his tax cuts are aimed at the class of people that don't need that kind of help.

Rutland Herald, January 5, 2003

———

Ninety-eight percent of the people got a very small benefit. Two percent got an enormous benefit.

Meet the Press, July 21, 2002

———

On the Campaign

For me to have to know right now, participating in the Democratic Party, how many troops are actively on duty in the United States military when that is actually a number that's composed both of people on duty today and people who are National Guard people who are on duty today, it's silly. That's like asking me who the ambassador to Rwanda is.

Meet the Press, June 22, 2003

———

I see ourselves as someone with a big surge, but I don't think we have cemented our position as the frontrunner at this point. We're prepared for all of the attacks we're going to get. Clearly, now, the shoe is on the other foot and they are going to come after me.

The Washington Post, August 23, 2003

———

There is an enormous desire for people to be told the straight truth about why things are a problem and what ought to be done different.

The Burlington Free Press, May 24, 2002

———

Seeing all those people [at the August 2003 Seattle rally], the enormity of it all really struck me. For the first time, I realized what it really means to be president of the United States—seeing all those people out there, counting on you.

The Stranger, August 28, 2003

———

This campaign's a little different from most campaigns in the sense that it's not really about me, it's about a movement to take back the country.

LA Weekly, August 29, 2003

———

I put one foot in front of me every day, and I try not to look at the nominating convention. That's a waste of time. I know the things I have to do tomorrow. That's enough for now.

The Boston Globe Magazine, November 24, 2002

———

It's more fun than hotels. To stay up yakking with somebody until a ridiculous hour when you have to get up at five in the morning, that's something I like. [Besides], it saves money.

On his penchant for staying at supporters' homes instead of hotels
USA Today, September 2, 2002

———

I'm probably not going to change a lot, because what we're doing is working. And I think if you try to mold yourself to be somebody you're not, that's when you lose.

Slate, July 28, 2003

———

It's true you have to listen to people who give you money in campaigns, but it's also true you don't have to do what they want.

The Nation, March 31, 2003

———

The part I like best about running for president is the same thing I like about campaigning in Vermont. When you get out in this country, you find with a few exceptions, that most people are pretty good people. They're good people, they're straightforward people, they're thoughtful people, and pretty well-educated about the issues.

Barre–Montpelier Vermont "The Times Argus,"
November 24, 2002

———

You can't focus on just one state at a time. It goes so fast that if you're not ready ahead of time, you're dead.

USA Today, August 25, 2003

———

The biggest lie people like me tell people like you at election time is, if you vote for me, I'll solve all your problems. The truth is, the power to change this country is in your hands, not mine. You have the power to take this party back and make it stand for something again.

The Stranger, August 28, 2003

My campaign is not about worrying about which interest groups I have to cater to. My campaign is about laying out a vision for the country and convincing people that this is in all of our best interests.

San Francisco Chronicle, October 19, 2002

[In the wake of passing the civil unions bill], being called a child molester and queer was great training for a presidential campaign. Given some of the things the Republicans do, what the right wing does on a national level, I figured now that I had a taste of it, I was ready to run.

New York Magazine, February 24, 2003

17

———

A campaign of hope beats a campaign of fear every time.

Newsweek, August 11, 2003

———

If those guys go for Kerry before I even get to see them, I'm going to hit the ceiling.

Dean on big-money donors
New York Magazine, February 24, 2003

———

There are two big issues in this campaign: national security and economic security.

Toledo Blade, August 25, 2003

———

I was a hands-on governor, I always knew what was going on in most areas and details of state government. When you're running for president, you have to put your fate in other people's hands. I don't have a lot of input into the scheduling, and a lot of times I get up in the morning and go where I'm told. They don't tell me what to *do*. Nobody can do that.

LA Weekly, August 29, 2003

———

On Campaign Finance Reform

I think public financing of a campaign is important, but I also have been in a position where I have opted out for practical reasons.

Salon, August 15, 2003

———

On Changing His Mind

I don't make any bones about switching my positions. In fact, that's what's wrong with this current administration—they won't admit when they are wrong despite the facts.

Brattleboro Reformer, September 1, 2002

———

On Civil Liberties

[The terrorist attacks] require a reevaluation of the importance of some of our specific civil liberties.

Associated Press, September 13, 2001

———

On Civil Unions

What I will do as president of the United States is insist that every state find a way to recognize the same legal rights for gay couples as they do for everybody else.

Meet the Press, June 22, 2003

———

Once in a generation, an issue comes along where there can be no compromise when you either have to figure out, do I stand up for the principles I believe in or am I simply keeping this seat warm?

Rutland Herald, January 27, 2002

———

At one of the first events I went to after the Civil Unions Act [was signed], I was a little startled when a guy came up and told me, "I must say, Governor, you're a very attractive man."

LA Weekly, August 29, 2003

———

The only people who call civil unions "gay marriage" are poorly informed reporters and the right wing of the Republican Party.

New York Magazine, February 24, 2003

———

I'm uncomfortable [with gay marriage], just like anybody else.

Out in the Mountains, June 2000

———

I think civil unions will continue to sweep across the country. As president, I would recognize civil unions federally, because equal rights under the law doesn't just mean equal rights under state law. It means equal rights under federal law.

San Francisco Chronicle, October 19, 2002

———

This is not a vote that is about politics. This is a vote that is about principle, and that principle is respect for everyone—and that is regardless of gender, ethnicity, sexual orientation, race, or any one of a number of factors that makes us different.

The Advocate, May 23, 2003

———

It was a very painful, difficult discussion to do this in the state of Vermont. And it's probably a painful, difficult discussion we have to have nationally. This is not an issue that is going to go away.

Meet the Press, July 21, 2002

———

For me as a political figure, it was in many ways the most important event in my political life. There aren't many people who get to do what I did.

Rutland Herald, January 27, 2002

———

[Civil unions] was one of the things that first got me thinking about a presidential bid. I realized that if I could get through the 2000 [post–civil union gubernatorial] election, I could certainly handle what the Republicans could throw at me nationally. I had no doubt about the righteousness of the cause and wanted to help take it to the rest of the country.

The Advocate, April 1, 2003

———

I think there is an increasing understanding that homosexuality is not chosen and that gay and lesbian people have the same rights and privileges of any members of society.

The Advocate, May 23, 2000

———

The gay and lesbian community has consistently been grateful. Usually in politics you struggle to do something for somebody, and the people who are helped by

it quickly assimilate into their normal life and they for-
get about it. I was deeply touched by how many people
came up to me to shake my hand and thank me.

Out in the Mountains, June 2000

On the Death Penalty

The only three instances that I support the death
penalty are, one, murder of a child, two, a mass murder
like a terrorist, and three, the shooting of a police officer.

Meet the Press, June 22, 2003

I was an opponent of capital punishment until the Polly
Klaas case. Then I realized that without capital punishment sometimes innocent life is lost. People get out of
jail on technicalities and then do it again. I just think
that people who murder children cannot be rehabili-
tated.

Texas Triangle, March 28, 2003

———

On the Democratic Party

I'm Howard Dean, and I'm here to represent the Democratic wing of the Democratic Party.

> Standard stump speech line

———

When I say that a lot of Democrats are more mad at the Democrats than at the Republicans, I get a lot of nods.

> *The Washington Post*, July 6, 2003

———

Most Democrats want a candidate who will behave like a Democrat on issues, and I don't mean the radical left.

> *San Antonio Express-News*, September 27, 2002

———

The Democratic National Committee is a club in Washington, and they prefer one of their own [to run for president], but the problem with that is that one of their own isn't going to beat George Bush. You don't beat George Bush by trying to be Bush Lite.

Philadelphia Weekly, August 6, 2003

———

I think the party wasn't winning elections because we were too far to the left. Now I think the party has moved too far to the right.

The Progressive, May 2003

———

You know, it's your own party that is always the one that gets you. I certainly had my hands full with my own party.

Barre–Montpelier Vermont "The Times Argus,"
November 24, 2002

27

———

I'm the non-Washington candidate. I'm going to run very hard against all the candidates who are inside the Beltway from Washington because I think they're going to have a hard time convincing the American people that somebody from Washington ought to beat this president.

Meet the Press, June 22, 2003

———

What we need to do is set up a Democratic agenda: unambiguous, clear, proud to be Democrats. If you put the Democratic agenda next to the Republican agenda, the Democratic agenda wins every time.

Barre–Montpelier Vermont "The Times Argus," April 2, 2003

———

The time is now to present a very different vision and stop trying to "me too" the Republicans.

Salon, February 20, 2003

———

They're consumed by the notion that they have to win, whatever the cost is. And that's why they don't win.

Slate, July 28, 2003

———

The problem is that we don't seem to know who we are.

The Nation, March 31, 2003

———

Too many Democrats in Washington have become so afraid of losing that they have remained silent, or only halfheartedly fought the very agenda that is destroying the democratic dream of America.

The Washington Post, July 31, 2003

———

On Drug Policy

The reason I don't support legalization or decriminal-
ization is because we already have enough trouble with
the two drugs that are legal: tobacco and alcohol. And to
send a message to kids that this is okay is not healthy.

Philadelphia Weekly, August 6, 2003

———

We need to treat drugs as a public health problem.
That's difficult to do. We actually don't have a lot of drug
users in our jails; the ones we have in there are drug
users who are also dealers. Jail is not a particularly effective way to get people to stop using drugs: treatment is.

Democracy in Action, July 10, 2002

———

I don't think we should single out a particular drug for
approval through political means when we approve
other drugs through scientific means.

AlterNet.org, August 12, 2003

On the Economy

We need to make a genuine effort to start to balance the budget to restore investor confidence. The second thing I would do is to support the small-business community. They create more jobs than large businesses do, and they don't move their jobs offshore.

BusinessWeek Online, August 11, 2003

We do have to do something about the economy, and at the federal level you can't slavishly adhere to a balanced budget at all times. First things first: Get rid of the tax cuts for people making more than $300,000. If jobs are still a problem, you have to look at the infrastructure. If the economy is turning around, then you can look at balancing the budget.

The Nation, March 31, 2003

On Education

The single most important factor in how a child learns has less to do with the quality of the building, the computers or even the teachers. The most important predictor is the attitude in that child's home toward education. We must involve parents again; we must insist that they participate in their children's education.

"Improving Education," deanforamerica.com

———

We have got to stop thinking in two- and four- and six-year increments in this country, and start thinking in twenty-year increments if we want to do something for children.

The Stranger, August 28, 2003

———

Special ed is the albatross around the neck of every school board in the country. It's an enormous amount of money to a local school board. It's just crushing them.

[If the federal government funded special education], they would have a lot more money to consider whether they wanted more teachers' salaries, new computers, or a better school building.

Texas Triangle, March 28, 2003

———

We have to be very, very careful not to destroy the public school system with harebrained ideas like vouchers. It puts the white folks here, the black folks there, the Hispanics there, the Jews over here, the Catholics there, the Protestants there, the rich people here, the poor people there, and the last people left behind are the special ed kids because nobody wants them.

The Weekly Standard, August 14, 2002

———

I want to fully fund special ed and start to unravel some of the president's education bill, which is mostly a huge unfunded mandate. If you fully funded special ed, that alone would be the most significant thing that you could possibly do for education, give the local school boards more flexibility in terms of how to improve their schools.

Texas Triangle, March 28, 2003

—————

On education what is good for Texas, as this law is, may not be good for the rest of the country.

PoliticsNH.com, February 7, 2003

—————

"Every Child Left Behind."

What Dean calls the No Child Left Behind law

—————

On Energy Policy

[Regarding] a renewable energy policy, I'm not talking about anything radical. I'm talking about if you simply apply the same mileage standards to include SUVs and trucks, you could save the entire amount of oil that is reputed to be in the Arctic National Wildlife Refuge in a single year. If we did that we would reduce our dependence on Saudi Arabia dramatically. Secondly, we ought to use 10 percent ethanol in every gasoline plant in the entire country.

Texas Triangle, March 28, 2003

―――――

On the Environment

In the long run the most critical environmental issue we face is renewable energy. Without it we risk drastically changing the climate of the earth and changing the lifestyle of every American and every person in the world.

Vermont Public Radio report, August 22, 2003

―――――

We've got to start thinking in hundred-year increments if we want to preserve the environment of this country and of this world. We need a president who doesn't think a renewable energy policy consists of drilling in the Arctic National Wildlife Refuge.

The Stranger, August 28, 2003

———

Environmental policy cannot be separated from other issues such as energy, trade, or economic policy. This is one reason that I will ask Congress to elevate the Environmental Protection Agency to cabinet status immediately.

"Environmental Report," deanforamerica.com

———

There're always those on the extreme edge of the right who want to clear-cut everything. That's their idea of sustainable timbering.

La Weekly, August 29, 2003

———

On the European Union

In a short period of time, the most dangerous continent on earth has been made into the most stable.

The Guardian, August 27, 2002

———

On the Far Right

I think the country's being run now by ideologues of the right. They can't tolerate ambiguity, and without ambiguity the world can't survive.

The Boston Globe Magazine, November 24, 2002

———

I don't think the religious right and I have much in common, and I wouldn't expect them to vote for many Democrats. We do have some things in common. I don't like gambling very much. But I fully expect a huge assault from the president's part of the party.

Texas Triangle, March 28, 2003

————

I'm tired of being bullied by the right wing. We're going to bring this country back to the middle. Our president has taken us so far to the right, we've forgotten what the middle looks like.

Iowa City Press-Citizen, September 24, 2002

————

On Foreign Policy

America has withdrawn from the world and we, for our own national security and defense policy, ought to be building societies and not the opposite.

Meet the Press, July 21, 2002

————

I'm tired of a foreign policy that says, basically, "Get out of my way or I'll see you in the parking lot after school."

The Stranger, May 15, 2003

———

There are a lot of evil men running around the world and we can't bomb every one of them.

Grand Forks Herald, September 16, 2002

———

I don't even think we can successfully nation-build in Afghanistan unless we have the Turks and the Germans and other folks helping us out.

Texas Triangle, March 28, 2003

———

The threshold for what America does militarily has got to be higher than anyone else's. America has always set the moral tone in foreign policy. And if we attack a nation unilaterally that's not a threat to us, it means that someone will try the same thing somewhere down the line and justify it by our actions.

The Washington Post, March 19, 2003

———

Renewable energy is very much a part of foreign policy, and you know, we paid al Qaeda essentially to blow us up. Because the money went to the Saudis, the Saudis bought off the radical Islamists, and they, of course, trained people to hate Christians, Jews, and Americans.

Texas Triangle, March 28, 2003

———

Our founders implored that we were not to be the new Rome. We are not to conquer and suppress other nations.

The Washington Post, June 24, 2003

———

The Marshall Plan was the most effective foreign policy initiative ever undertaken by the United States and possibly by any nation. It proved that what you get for your money in nation-building is peace, stability, and allies.

Texas Triangle, March 28, 2003

———

On Gun Control

This is a state issue. Keep the federal laws. Enforce them vigorously. And then let every state decide what they want. When you say gun control in my state, people are going to think you're taking the squirrel rifle their parents gave them away.

Meet the Press, June 22, 2003

———

I've never met a hunter who thought he needed an AK-47 to shoot a deer.

Philadelphia Weekly, August 6, 2003

———

[In Vermont] there are only two gun laws: you can't bring a loaded gun to school, and you can't have a loaded gun in the car. We don't want people to shoot deer out of the window of a moving car; we don't think that's fair for the deer.

New York Magazine, February 24, 2003

———

When I go to South Carolina and Tennessee, I'm not going to have the baggage Al Gore had because I'm not going to make gun control a big issue in my campaign.

PoliticsNJ.com, June 6, 2002

———

I support the assault-weapon ban, I support the Brady Bill. I want to close the gun-show loophole. But after that, I want each state to be able to make their own gun laws, as much as they want or as little as they want.

The Progressive, May 2003

———

If Al Gore had taken the position that I take, he'd be sitting in the White House right now. One could argue that I'm the most electable of all the Democrats because I'm the only one who hasn't taken on the position that we ought to have lots of gun control in this country.

Boston Phoenix, December 19, 2002

———

I do support closing the gun-show loophole, but I would like to see InstaCheck, which is the same system that we have elsewhere, and I think if it takes keeping somebody on duty in law enforcement agencies [on weekends], that would be fine.

Meet the Press, July 21, 2002

———

Additional gun control ought to be done on a state-by-state basis . . . we ought not to have a one-size-fits-all federal government approach.

Meet the Press, July 21, 2002

———

Democrats are getting killed on gun control. Democratic activists who basically are in favor of gun control are glad to see me coming in the West and the South, because they do not want to lose any more national elections on the gun issue.

Meet the Press, July 21, 2002

On Health Care Reform

All [we want to do] is expand the current system. I learned in 1993 that reforming the system is not likely to pass because the interest groups will kill it, and then 42 million people are left without insurance. What I'm interested in is getting something passed to expand the existing system to cover everybody.

Philadelphia Weekly, August 6, 2003

———

I don't want another Harry and Louise campaign.

Vermont Public Radio news report, March 20, 2003

———

If you can guarantee health insurance for all Americans, that takes away a need that a lot of people at the top get and a lot of people at the bottom don't.

Democracy in Action, July 10, 2002

———

There are going to have to be significant deductibles
and co-payments. The idea is not to make sure that
nobody ever pays another nickel out of their pockets for
health care. The idea is to make sure that people don't
go bankrupt.

Texas Triangle, March 28, 2003

———

Harry Truman first introduced the notion of health
insurance for all Americans in 1948. Now people consider it a socialist plot. That shows how far to the right
we are. I think it's too far right, and I think most Americans agree with that.

The Progressive, May 2003

———

As a doctor, I think I'm in the most unique position to
deliver health insurance to the American people. If I get
elected I'm going to do it in my first term.

Stateline.org, July 9, 2002

———

The mistake [the Clintons] made was that they tried to reform health care and improve access at the same time. The first thing you do is create access. Once you get everybody in the system, then you can fight about reforming it.

The Boston Globe Magazine, November 24, 2002

———

This is not a Cadillac health insurance program. It's a catastrophic health insurance program with first-dollar coverage for things like colonoscopies and mammograms that nobody would get if they had to pay for them. But after that, there's a big deductible.

The Nation, March 31, 2003

———

We can't promise seniors everything, but we can promise them that nobody's ever going to have to choose between paying their rent and getting the medications they need to live.

Concord Monitor, January 24, 2003

———

My plan is not reform. If you want to totally change the health care system, I'm not your guy. I'm not interested in having a big argument about what the best system is. I'm interested in getting everybody covered.

The New York Times, July 30, 2003

———

On His Family

I feel very strongly that you do not drag the rest of your family along in your political career and use them as props. It's important to make sure you have a good, strong marriage, and that means having both of us doing things that really reward us in life. There'll be some controversy about it. Some people will say she [Judith] should be out there.

The Washington Post, November 25, 2002

———

47

On His Opponents

[Lieberman] is coming after me on policy differences, which is fine. I think some of the others might be a little less highbrow about it. We'll find out.

The Washington Post, August 23, 2003

———

We expect to be attacked, of course. We'll deal with that when we get there.

The Stranger, August 28, 2003

———

I wish [Senator Kerry] would say to my face what he says behind my back.

Bennington Banner, September 6, 2003

———

I'm going to be called all kinds of things in this campaign, and the better I do, the worse things I'm going to be called.

Meet the Press, July 21, 2002

———

My tactics are different from everybody in the race. [My Democratic opponents] kind of do the traditional Washington things and trim on the margins. I don't think we can win that way.

The Stranger, May 15, 2003

———

On His Past

I'm going to take the Bush approach. My exuberant youth was my exuberant youth and it has no relevance toward the presidency. What was very funny when you were eighteen wasn't very funny when you're thirty.

Salon, February 20, 2003

———

I had long hair. My drug of choice was beer. I didn't generally engage in an excessive lifestyle. I mean, you know, I dabbled in a little of this and a little of that. We did some heavy-duty partying, but I didn't do anything outrageous.

U.S. News & World Report, August 11, 2003

———

On His Sudden Popularity

If you'd asked me six months ago would I be in the position I am today, I would have said, "Don't be ridiculous." We've caught fire and, frankly, not with anything we've done that's so brilliant. I wish we were so smart to have figured out the Internet thing, but the fact is, the Internet community found us.

Newsweek, August 11, 2003

———

We're doing much better than I ever expected we would do this early. I expected to do well, but not this early. And it has caused us to change the campaign. We had to move out of our campaign office and give up four or five months on our lease because we just didn't have enough room.

The Stranger, August 28, 2003

———

I have no right to be where I am if you look at this race on paper. The reason I am where I am is because I say what I think.

The New York Times, July 30, 2003

———

On His Temperament

I have to be blunt. It's what will differentiate me from the others. Blunt is what I do. I think there's an enormous market for somebody who says what he thinks.

The Boston Globe Magazine, November 24, 2002

———

What those guys don't understand about me is that getting me mad is a bad thing to do. My instincts are not to take off the gloves. And the reason I do is that people say things like [calling me antiwar] and it gets me mad.

The Washington Post, March 19, 2003

———

I do have a mouth on me. I can get snippy, no doubt about it.

Bennington Banner, September 6, 2003

I can be overbearing to people whose ideas I don't agree with or respect.

National Journal, November 23, 2002

I'll probably dispense with some of the more rhetorical flourishes. One time I said the Supreme Court is so far right you couldn't see it anymore. Next summer I won't be talking like that. It's true and I'm not ashamed to have said it, but it doesn't sound very presidential.

Salon, February 20, 2003

On His Tenure as Governor of Vermont

You never get everything that you want in a bill. I've been a governor for eleven years. I've never yet signed a bill where I liked every little piece of it.

Meet the Press, July 21, 2002

———

The reason I was so successful as a governor is that early on I stood up to members of my own party who wanted to tax and spend, and I said no. And then Independents and moderate Republicans started to trust me.

The Stranger, May 15, 2003

———

The 2000 campaign was a tough one because there was so much anger over civil unions. In some ways that was the most rewarding campaign, because I was almost put back in the role of being doctor again. I knew what I had to do, and it was not about politics, it was about medicine—you have to listen to people. I knew people were mad at me and I just went around and listened to people and let them say terrible things at me for awhile.

Barre–Montpelier Vermont "The Times Argus,"
November 24, 2002

As governor of Vermont, I've stood up for a lot of things I believed in that people didn't think were a good idea. We did 'em anyway and I always got reelected.

Salon, February 20, 2003

There's a certain connection between a governor and the American people that doesn't exist if you're from Washington. My job has been so different for the last eleven years that I have an ability to really connect with people in a very no-nonsense way, which governors have to do.

Stateline.org, July 9, 2002

I don't get to do just what I want in this job. I'm hired to make sure that I can do what the boss wants and the boss is two hundred thousand voters.

Democracy in Action, July 10, 2002

———

I vetoed more bills in the history of the state than anyone else, and I never was overridden. Some of the
vetoes I regret, they were really more petulant than
based in fact. These were small bills that didn't mean
much, but I was just angry with [the liberal wing of the
party] and trying to prove a point.

Salon, February 20, 2003

———

I always believed in the end your job as governor tran-
scended your party and that is a test for every governor.

Barre–Montpelier Vermont "The Times Argus,"
November 24, 2002

———

One of the advantages I have is I was governor for so
long in Vermont that I actually served through both
Bush recessions, not one of them.

Dean implying voting for Bush means voting for recession
NPR's *Day to Day,* July 29, 2003

On Homeland Security

I think the federal government has been very good about homeland security. I don't have any complaints. Maybe a few small ones, but nothing significant. They've come up with some money that we need. They're serious about it.

Stateline.org, July 9, 2002

Homeland security is nothing but a bureaucratic shuffle so far. There's too much emphasis on duct tape and plastic.

Nashua Telegraph, February 17, 2003

On How People Perceive Him

I think being likable is a big deal. Part of that likability stuff is not having a big smile and a glad hand; it's about having people respect you.

U.S. News & World Report, August 11, 2003

———

Most people don't think I'm brusque.

The Washington Post, August 4, 2003

———

People have no idea what kind of politician I am because they have no idea what governing Vermont is like for the most part, because they've never come up and seen it.

Slate, July 28, 2003

———

When I admit I don't know something, everyone in Washington says, "Oh my God, can you believe he said that?"

The Washington Post, July 1, 2003

———

On How to Win the Election

The way to beat this president is not to be like him.

AP Online, August 26, 2003

———

We're going to beat this president by giving the 50 percent of Americans who've given up on voting a reason to vote again.

The Stranger, August 28, 2003

———

I truly, honestly believe that my directness and my unwillingness to bend for the most part for political reasons is going to be a quality that I'm going to have the corner on the market on out there.

Burlington Free Press, May 24, 2002

———

Beating George Bush is not going to be an easy task. For someone to beat him, two things have got to happen. He's got to be in trouble on the economy, and there has to be an alternative that's credible. [Then], it's a very winnable race.

Texas Triangle, March 28, 2003

———

I don't think we can beat George Bush with someone from inside Washington.

The Advocate, April 1, 2003

———

How can a guy from a state with six hundred thousand people and three electoral votes win this? I'm going to get out and work my fanny off, and I'm very forthright.

PoliticsNJ.com, June 6, 2002

———

Be proud of who you are and stand up for what you are and who you are, and that's how we can beat George Bush. And I don't think the other guys from Washington are going to be able to do that.

Meet the Press, June 22, 2003

———

My whole theory about how to beat George Bush is different than the other guys from Washington. My theory is instead of trying to get yourself in the middle of the ever-shrinking rightward-moving electorate, try to motivate new people to vote.

Vermont Public Radio news report, August 4, 2003

61

———

How is the Democratic governor of the forty-ninth-largest state going to beat George Bush? George W. Bush is a borrow-and-spend liberal, and I tell people that I'm going to beat George W. Bush by running to his right.

The Boston Globe Magazine, November 24, 2002

———

The president's not popular because of his issues, so we should stop co-opting those issues. The president's popular because people think he's a strong leader. That's what you have to get by in order to become president.

Slate, July 28, 2003

———

The only way to beat George Bush is to run a really tough, hard-hitting campaign and let the American people know what we're doing. And that's why we started as early as we did.

USA Today, August 25, 2003

No Democrat has a chance of winning in 2004 if the economy is good.

National Journal, November 23, 2002

On Immigration

I believe that if you've worked here for a period of time and you've paid your taxes and you don't have a criminal record, you should be on a fast track for citizenship.

Arizona Daily Sun, September 6, 2003

On Iraq

I'm the only one of the four elected officials running at this point who did not support the president's Iraq resolution—and I still don't.

New York Magazine, February 24, 2003

63

———

I see Iraq as a country that we've successfully contained for twelve years and can contain indefinitely. It's a third-rate military power which poses dangers to those in the region, which is why I think they ought to be disarmed, but not by the United States.

Vermont Public Radio news report, March 20, 2003

———

We have to be honest about how long we're going to be there. We're going to have American troops on the ground in Iraq for ten years.

Rutland Herald, August 21, 2002

———

The wrong war at the wrong time.

The Stranger, May 15, 2003

———

Sooner or later somebody else, perhaps the Chinese, will say, "Taiwan is a threat, so let's go in. And the United States has done it, so why don't we have the right to do it?"

Rutland Herald, March 3, 2003

———

What I want to know is why in the world the Democratic Party leadership is supporting the president's unilateral attack on Iraq.

U.S. News & World Report, August 11, 2003

———

On Israel

I recognize both the special relationship the United States has with Israel and the legitimate claim of the Palestinian people to a state of their own. I believe agreements satisfying both sides can be reached leading to two states living side by side in peace. To get there,

65

Palestinians will have to crack down on terror and take real steps to make democracy work, while Israel will have to give up some settlements and ensure that the Palestinian quality of life improves.

The Forward, August 22, 2003

———

I have hope for the Israel and Palestine situation. The biggest problem is terror. The United States plays a major role in stopping the terror and brokering a solution.

Iowa City Press-Citizen, January 20, 2003

———

At one time the Peace Now view was important, but now Israel is under enormous pressure. We have to stop terrorism before peace negotiations.

The Forward, November 22, 2002

———

I don't think you can pressure the Israelis to do anything until you stop the terror.

The Nation, March 31, 2003

———

On the Kyoto Treaty

It doesn't require the underdeveloped countries to do anything about greenhouse gases and would have the effect of moving the steel industry or other industries that pollute into countries where there are no requirements to improve their situation with greenhouse gases.

The Nation, March 31, 2003

———

On Labor and Unions

Federal labor law should be amended to declare that a union is established whenever a majority of workers have signed cards stating that they wish to unionize.

This would avoid protracted and divisive campaigns in which employers use intimidation and coercion to block unionization.

"Supporting America's Workers," deanforamerica.com

———

On Leadership

You've got to have long-term vision and then you've got to be willing to take short incremental steps to get to the long-term vision, and then you've got to also explain to people sometimes why they have to do things that they don't want to do and get them to do it. But you also have to listen to people and figure out what it is they want to do and figure out how to get them what they want.

Democracy in Action, July 10, 2002

———

On the Media

I don't get to see myself on television. On the talk shows, I'm not strident. When I'm giving speeches, I get very passionate.

Slate, July 28, 2003

———

The press tends to focus on all the worst news and they rarely print the good news, and that's part of the problem.

Rutland Herald, July 8, 2002

———

I'm not at all pretentious. So it's easier for writers to make some assessment of who I am, and it's easy for them to kind of see behind the curtain. It makes it easier to interview me and more fun, I think, for them.

National Journal, November 23, 2002

———

People really do get a sense of who you are through the media. And I agree that the media manipulates this and that and the other thing but in the long run I think people have a sense of who you are. Now if you make a lot of mistakes, you know people are going to be trying to spin you and you've got to be willing to fight back.

Democracy in Action, July 10, 2002

———

It's shorthand. The press does it all the time and I don't say anything about it, but it's shorthand. It pigeonholes you, and I don't think that's what the press's job is. It makes me think of someone who's just trying to rush through and get home for dinner on time.

Salon, February 20, 2003

———

I tend to get brusque and tough with the press. When they push me, I push back vigorously. But I never behave like that with ordinary Americans. They never see the side of me that aggressive reporters or aggressive editorial boards see.

The Washington Post, August 4, 2003

———

Where do you dig these people up? Do you have anybody who likes me that you've quoted?

To a reporter who asked Dean's opinion on Vermont politicians

Democracy in Action, July 10, 2002

———

I'm very mindful of what happened to John Edwards. You all created him, and then you all cut his legs out from under him.

Dean talking about the media's flavor-of-the-week mentality

The Washington Post, July 1, 2003

On Medicinal Marijuana

I hate the idea of legislators and politicians practicing medicine.

The Nation, March 31, 2003

I will require the FDA to evaluate marijuana with a double-blind study with the same kinds of scientific protocols that every other drug goes through. I'm certainly willing to abide by what the FDA says.

AlterNet.org, August 12, 2003

On the Military

I will never hesitate to send troops anywhere in the world to defend our country, but I will never send our sons and daughters to die in a foreign country without telling the truth to the American people about why they are there.

USA Today, August 25, 2003

———

If we don't begin to use diplomacy as part of our foreign policy, we won't always have the strongest military.

Meet the Press, June 22, 2003

———

I don't think you can cut the defense budget. First of all, we're in a time where we need a strong defense, and second there are too many shortcomings in intelligence and a lot of salary and benefit issues [for military personnel].

BusinessWeek Online, August 11, 2003

———

On NAFTA

Prices will go up. But so what? In return, you've fixed the illegal immigration problem, you've fixed the drain of jobs problem, you've created a middle class that can buy American exports. There's a lot you get for that.

Slate, July 28, 2003

———

I think free trade has been good because it opens the possibility of middle-class livelihoods for developing countries, and that's good for national security. But in the long run those countries have got to unionize their workforce and comply with world environmental standards. Otherwise, they'll have industrial capacity but they won't have the capacity to develop into a middle-class country.

Texas Triangle, March 28, 2003

———

On New Yorkers

New Yorkers are tough. They want to know what you've got. But I've never had people open their hearts to me more than when they discover that my wife is Jewish and I'm from New York. They look at you completely differently. It's flabbergasting.

New York Magazine, February 24, 2003

———

On North Korea

North Korea is about to become a nuclear power because (Bush) won't sit down and talk to somebody he doesn't like. If you want to be tough on defense, you have to do better than a foreign policy based on petulance.

AP Online, August 23, 2003

———

On the Other Candidates

I think it's important that all of us are out there. I mean, it's really like five of us being able to go after the president's record at once. I think that's a good opportunity for the Democrats.

Stateline.org, July 9, 2002

———

If you as a Democrat are willing to vote with the president, the most conservative president in our lifetime, 85 percent of the time, then why not vote for the [Republican] who is going to vote for the president 100 percent of the time, which is what [the other candidates] did.

Barre–Montpelier Vermont "The Times Argus," April 2, 2003

———

Our candidates think the best way to get elected is to talk to everybody about voting for things like the leave-every-school-board-behind education bill, which is going to cost the New Hampshire taxpayers $109 million. I can't wait for those four guys from Congress to come up here and explain to us why they wanted to raise your property taxes after they supported a tax cut for the wealthiest people in America.

Concord Monitor, January 24, 2003

On the Patriot Act

There are a number of things in the Patriot Act that are unconstitutional. One is the idea of being able to search through library records without a proper warrant. Two is the idea of being able to search through video store records without a warrant. Three is incarceration of American citizens without access to a lawyer. I'll ask Congress to revise the Patriot Act and take out the things that are clearly an invasion of individual privacy.

Philadelphia Weekly, August 6, 2003

They went too far. I had no idea they were going to take away the ability of an American to get a lawyer if they get arrested for something. What I had in mind was allowing my bags to be searched at the airport.

MSNBC, August 8, 2003

On Politics

One of the things I learned early on was to try not to spend a lot of political capital on turf battles. What we do in Vermont to try and get around the type of problems that the president has with homeland security is simply to put somebody in the governor's office and force the agencies to report to them and work together. And if they don't do it, we just find new people to run the agency.

Texas Triangle, March 28, 2003

Ninety-nine percent of politics is about resource allocation. We argue over money. We can fight over money, and then we can compromise.

Meet the Press, July 21, 2002

On the Presidency

[People] give you wide latitude on the issues if they like the way you make decisions.

The New York Times, July 30, 2003

———

The one I would like to emulate the most is Harry Truman, because I think he was very no-nonsense, and he took the tough positions that were the best for America, that weren't particularly popular at the time.

Texas Triangle, March 28, 2003

———

Nobody can run for president without being willing to use the full and maximum power of the United States. But I'm one president who would be very careful if I had the opportunity.

New York Magazine, February 24, 2003

———

On President George W. Bush

I like the president. He's an engaging person, but I think for some reason he's been captured by the neo-conservatives around him.

U.S. News & World Report, August 11, 2003

George Bush governed Texas as a relative moderate—not a super moderate—but then when he came into the White House he started espousing all this super right-wing stuff.

The Progressive, May 2003

He's a healing personality, certainly a very pleasant person, but he's at the far end of the political spectrum and so he has an agenda that he has to advance and sort of a base with a lot of hateful people in it that he serves from time to time. So he can say all the nice things he wants about compassionate conservatism, but his agenda is not a compassionate agenda; it can't be by definition.

Democracy in Action, July 10, 2002

———

I believed [Bush] when he said he was going to be a compassionate conservative. I believed him when he said he was going to increase AmeriCorps. The only thing the president has kept his word on, as far as I can see, is he said he was going to invade Iraq.

Slate, July 28, 2003

———

Has anybody really stood up against George Bush and his policies? Don't you think it's time somebody did?

U.S. News & World Report, August 11, 2003

———

I've seen others criticize the president. I think it's very easy to second-guess the commander in chief at a time of war. I don't choose to engage in doing that.

Meet the Press, July 21, 2002

———

On the President He'd Be

[I'd] stop giving monopolies to big radio station owners who kick the Dixie Chicks off the air because they don't agree with their political philosophy.

The Stranger, May 15, 2003

———

Most governors believe that the relationship between the governor and the legislature is somehow similar to the relationship between the president and Congress. Which isn't true. Congress is much more powerful than the president in some ways. So I think clearly what you don't do is bring all your home people from your home state to run the country. What you have to do is recruit people who know how to get things done in Washington.

Texas Triangle, March 28, 2003

———

I'll tell people not what they want to hear, but what they need to hear.

The New Republic, July 1, 2002

———

If you make me president of the United States, I will restore the honor and dignity and the respect for this country that we deserve in the world by having high moral purpose.

The Stranger, August 28, 2003

———

Running a government in good times and keeping the money so that in the bad times, as we're seeing now, so you don't have to cut education and social welfare and have kids not getting the health care they need.

MSNBC, August 8, 2003

———

On Prison Reform

You know, a kindergarten teacher can tell you the five kids in her class who are most likely to end up in jail. What we've done in Vermont is do hospital visits to every mom. Then we follow up at home two weeks later. We identify an enormous number of kids who are probably going to get in trouble, and we give the parents lots of services and lots of help. We've dropped our child abuse rate 43 percent in the last ten years and we've dropped our child sexual abuse rate 70 percent.

Texas Triangle, March 28, 2003

———

On Race

I grew up in New York. I've spent time in fifty different countries over the course of my life, which I suspect is more countries than the current inhabitant of the White House will have been to by November of the election year. I think that I'll be able to deal with the issue of full minority participation in America, which is really what Democrats have already stood for.

Meet the Press, July 21, 2002

———

"Quota" is a racially loaded word designed to divide people by race.

The Stranger, May 15, 2003

———

On Reproductive Rights

As a doctor, I feel very strongly that Congress and the president and legislatures and governors have no business practicing medicine. I believe that abortion is a matter between a woman, between her physician and her family and it is none of the government's business.

Meet the Press, July 21, 2002

———

On Republicans

New England Republicans are not the same as the right-wing wackos in Washington.

The Boston Globe, June 23, 2003

———

Republicans have turned into tax-and-spend liberals.

Portsmouth Herald, September 28, 2002

———

We better have a Democratic president because Republicans can't handle money.

Iowa City Press-Citizen, January 20, 2003

———

On the Role of Government

Capitalism is a great system, and to make it work you must have social justice. But it's all in the balancing. Government is the mediator.

The Washington Post, August 3, 2003

———

On Rural States

Democrats are never going to be president again unless we can win in small, rural states.

Grand Forks Herald, September 16, 2002

———

You can't revitalize rural America unless you preserve and protect the family farm. And you can't preserve and protect the family farm unless you revitalize rural America. The two issues go hand in hand.

"Restoring Rural Communities" speech, August 13, 2003

———

Farmers want to make their living from the market, not from farm programs.

"Restoring Rural Communities" speech, August 13, 2003

———

On Saudi Arabia

Our oil money goes to the Saudis, where it is recycled and some of it is recycled to Hamas and to fundamentalist schools which teach small children to hate Americans, Christians, and Jews. This president will not confront the Saudis.

The Washington Post, August 23, 2003

On Small Business

[We need] to start focusing on American-created small businesses, because corporations have become international citizens and not national citizens any longer. And you just can't count on American corporations standing up for American workers any more. And I don't say that in a bad way. Corporations pay great wages and we want them here in Vermont. What I mean is that they have a responsibility to their shareholders. And if they have to move to China, they'll do it.

Rutland Herald, July 15, 2002

On Smallpox Vaccinations

I think it's very unlikely that smallpox will be used as an agent, but I think the country is proper to be prepared for that eventuality. I would not vaccinate every American, but I do believe first responders should be vaccinated.

Meet the Press, July 21, 2002

On Social Security

The best way to balance the Social Security budget right now is to expand the amount of money that Social Security payroll taxes apply to. It's limited now to something like $80,000. You let that rise.

Meet the Press, June 22, 2003

On Taking the Middle Road

I really have a healthy mistrust of the left as well as the right. I distrust ideologues and I distrust people who find facts inconvenient. My MO has been to be in the middle. Facts matter to me a lot, probably because of my scientific training. I simply don't trust the extremes on both ends.

The Nation, March 31, 2003

———

I just don't do well with ideologically motivated people, because I think that they all sacrifice people they care about for the ideologically motivated positions. I think people who are ideological are impatient with me because I don't really care about ideology very much.

The Stranger, May 15, 2003

———

The left always made me very suspicious. I certainly did not support the war, but I was mistrustful of people like Jerry Rubin and Abbie Hoffman, and very mistrustful of Students for a Democratic Society.

The New Republic, July 1, 2002

———

On Taxes

If you say should we get rid of the president's tax cuts, people are going to say "No," because they never want to get rid of a tax cut. But if you say the truth, which is you have a choice: you can have the president's tax cut or a prescription benefit, or you could fully fund special education, or a road budget could be restored. Most people are going to pick roads, education, and health care every single time.

Vermont Public Radio news report, April 21, 2003

———

On Terrorism

There is nothing that excuses terrorism, and terrorists ought to be prosecuted to the full extent of the American ability to do so. I think we're doing a fairly good job of it. We have to get populations to stop supporting terrorists.

Meet the Press, July 21, 2002

———

Initially [Bush] did very well. His pursuit of terrorists in Afghanistan was very good. But now, with Iraq, we're not going after terrorists, although he'd like to pretend we are.

Nashua Telegraph, February 17, 2003

———

I'd really go after the Saudis, the Iranians, and the Syrians to get them to stop funneling money for terrorism purposes.

Boston Phoenix, December 19, 2002

———

I don't think [terrorism] is a great political avenue to go down for the Democrats.

Des Moines Register, May 22, 2002

———

I think it's very unlikely atomic weapons are going to be used against us in a terrorist attack. I would be more concerned about a so-called dirty bomb.

Meet the Press, July 21, 2002

———

If September 11, 2001, taught America anything, it is that we are stronger when we are beholden to each other as a national community, and weaker when we act only as individuals.

"Great American Restoration" speech, June 23, 2003

———

On the United States Congress

Name one significant piece of legislation or social change in the last ten years that came from the Congress. There isn't one.

Boston Phoenix, December 19, 2002

———

On Urban Renewal

I want to double the Community Development Block Grant Program. And I want to invest in infrastructure, especially in the schools. For the cities, the principal investment would be the schools and to give cities more access to discretionary money to create jobs.

Philadelphia Weekly, August 6, 2003

On the Use of the Internet in His Campaign

It's an incredibly powerful weapon in our arsenal and we have had more help from folks communicating to each other. It's what put the campaign on the map. It's what's going to lead us to win and it's going to lead us to taking back the country.

Vermont Public Radio news report, April 21, 2003

———

On Vermont

I'm most proud of our fiscal stability. I left the state in better shape than I found it.

The Washington Post, August 3, 2003

———

I think people here feel pretty strongly that everybody is equal, and that includes the governor. The governor doesn't drive around in a limousine in this state, and there's a reason for that.

The Advocate, May 23, 2003

On Veterans

The president is a complete hypocrite when it comes to the veterans. He goes to a veterans' hospital and announces that they are going to have the best health care in the world. But in fact the day before, he cut the health care benefits of 164,000 veterans.

Philadelphia Weekly, August 6, 2003

[Bush] proposed cutting the pay of the people he sent to defend America in Iraq. We can do better than that. We ought to treat our veterans with respect in this country, and he's not doing it.

The Stranger, August 28, 2003

On War

Unilateral action is not appropriate unless there is an imminent threat to the United States.

The Nation, March 31, 2003

——

There is a fundamental difference between the defense of our nation and the doctrine of preemptive war espoused by this administration.

AlterNet.org, August 12, 2003

——

I supported the first Gulf War. I supported the invasion of Afghanistan because they killed three thousand of our people and I thought that was a matter of national defense.

Des Moines Register, August 16, 2003

———

Most people have no idea [of the destruction of war], except people who lost their kids in combat. That's why I think my fellow politicians running for the Democratic nomination are wrong [about supporting the war in Iraq].

Dean speaking of losing a brother in the Vietnam War
New York Magazine, February 24, 2003

———

On *The West Wing*

I think it's great. Who could be lucky enough to have their candidacy be on television every Wednesday night?

Boston Phoenix, December 19, 2002

———

On Who He Is

You can't move people unless you stand for something. When I get done with this campaign, I don't know if I'm going to win or lose, but everybody in America will know what I stood for.

New York Magazine, February 24, 2003

————

I'm not a terribly reflective person. I generally think about the future, not the past. I don't often look back at decisions I've made. I don't think, "If I only hadn't done this or if only I hadn't done that."

Barre–Montpelier Vermont "The Times Argus,"
November 24, 2002

————

I don't care what the polls say.

Boston Phoenix, December 19, 2002

99

———

My attitude is that if I say what I believe to be right, people will make their choice.

PoliticsNJ.com, June 6, 2002

———

I'm a fiscal conservative and a social progressive.

BusinessWeek Online, August 11, 2003

———

I'm very direct and very blunt. The pitch is that I'm different from every other candidate in the race. I'm a governor, I'm the only one who's ever balanced a budget, I'm the only one who doesn't support the president on Iraq. They can talk about health care; I've done it. They can talk about land conservation; I've done it. They can talk about early-childhood intervention; I've done it.

New York Magazine, February 24, 2003

———

[I have] a willingness to make tough decisions. To look at all of the facts, whether they are convenient or inconvenient, and the willingness to listen to other people's advice. An ability to talk to people directly without shading the truth. A willingness to deliver good news and bad news, and—this is a critical skill that is part of being a doctor—you have to deliver the bad news with a plan to get out of the situation.

The Washington Post, August 4, 2003

———

I don't speak well from prepared texts.

The Stranger, August 28, 2003

———

My philosophy is you just get your issues out there and the timing is something you don't have any control over.

Associated Press, February 24, 2002

———

I don't shy away from telling people my positions. In Washington, it pays you to blur the edges of issues. I can't do that as governor, and I won't do it as a presidential candidate.

The Washington Post, July 12, 2002

———

I will stand up for what I think is right no matter what the polls say.

The Advocate, April 1, 2003

———

Jimmy Carter is the reason that I got into politics, and I always admired his tenacity.

Stateline.org, July 9, 2002

———

Judy [my wife] and I don't care much about material things. My life isn't restaurants and theaters. It's skiing and hiking and camping.

New York Magazine, February 24, 2003

———

On Why He's Running for President

I want jobs again, which means you need a president who manages the economy. I want to get the universal health insurance into America that other industrialized countries have. But mostly I want a restoration of our sense of community, that we're all in this together.

Philadelphia Weekly, August 6, 2003

———

I'm in this race for two reasons: first of all, because I intend to win, and secondly, because I think I can move the party and the country whether I win or not. Obviously, I could move them a lot further if I win, but I don't get to make that choice. All I get to do is put my ideas out there and put me out there, and then we'll see how people respond.

Stateline.org, July 9, 2002

―――――

I was reading the paper and I was really furious at something the president had done, and I thought, "What're you going to do about it?"

The Boston Globe Magazine, November 24, 2002

―――――

I realized you could win by standing up for what you believe in.

The New York Times, July 30, 2003

One of the reasons I'm running is to bring a balanced budget to Washington, because I'm so appalled by the way the Republicans are managing the economy.

Meet the Press, July 21, 2002

It's not enough for me just to have good schools for my kid, or good health care for my kid. It's really important for us to provide these things for everybody. That's been the premise of America. That's what we have to get back again.

LA Weekly, August 29, 2003

On Working with His Legislative Colleagues

I've alienated them all at one time or another.

The Boston Globe Magazine, November 24, 2002

———

You've got your nuts on the left, your nuts on the right, and you've got me.

A phrase he frequently used with legislators,

according to state auditor Elizabeth Ready

The Washington Post, August 3, 2003

———

At home, people are always complaining when you leave. And one year I stayed in the legislature the whole time because they complained. Then they complained I was there too much.

Meet the Press, July 21, 2002